OBSCURE CLASSICS OF ENGLISH PROGRESSIVE ROCK

Poems by
Quincy R. Lehr

A SEVEN TOWERS PUBLICATION

First published 2012
By
Seven Towers 4, St Mura's Terrace,
Strangford Road, East Wall, Dublin 3, Ireland.

www.seventowers.ie

ISBN 978-0-9571510-4-8

Copyright © Quincy R. Lehr 2012

Cover, type, layout design and typesetting by
Seven Towers

Illustrations: Cover picture, works at South Docks taken from Bull Wall, Dublin; picture, page 10: St Doolagh's Church, Kinsealy, Dublin; picture, page 26, Malahide Castle grounds, Dublin; picture, page 36, *Before and After*, Tara Street, Dublin; picture, page 50, St Kevin's Monastery, Glendalough, Co. Wicklow; picture, page 58, Poolbeg Lighthouse, Great South Wall, Dublin.

Photographs © Sarah Lundberg

ACKNOWLEDGMENTS

I wrote the vast majority of the poems between 2007 and 2010 in Dublin, Galway, and Brooklyn, though a few are somewhat older pieces that simply had a long gestation.

Poems in this collection, or versions of them, have appeared in:

American Arts Quarterly (U.S.A.)—"Art House Cinema"
Angle (UK/Australia) - "Less than Expected"
The Barefoot Muse (U.S.A.)—"Suicide Town," "Jimmy Carter, King of America"
The Battered Suitcase (U.S.A.)—"Fragment from an American Folk Song, Circa. 2003," "The Rest of the Story," "The Year Zero"
Boyne Berries (Ireland)—"Masks"
Cadenza (UK)—"Homelands," "Heuston Station"
Chronogram (U.S.A.)—"The News Comes Every Morning"
The Dark Horse (UK)—"A Change of Season"
Crannóg (Ireland)—"If God Is Good," "It's Business"
The Flea (Australia)—"The Only Thing That Changes Is the Light"
Galway First (Ireland)—"We All Have Our Needs"
Grasp (Czech Republic)—"The Leap"
Literary House Review (U.S.A.)—"Brooklyn, 2008"
Measure (U.S.A.)—"No Snow Yet in Galway"
New Walk (UK)—"Ice Storm," "Ye Watchers and Ye Holy Ones"
Other Poetry (UK)—"Staying In"
The Raintown Review (U.S.A.)—"White Anglo-Saxon Protestant"
The Recusant (UK)—"Apartments"
Umbrella (U.S.A.)—"Minor Character"
and in the anthologies *Census: The First Seven Towers Anthology* ("Triptych") and *Census 2* ("Sceneshifts").
"We All Have Our Needs" won first prize in Tigh Neachtains' love sonnet contest, 14 February 2008.

— Quincy R. Lehr
Brooklyn, NY

In memory of Ray Pospisil

CONTENTS

SPACE IS DEEP

FRAGMENT FROM AN AMERICAN FOLK SONG, CIRCA. 2003

You're drunk and you're bored and you're slouching beneath
an unwatched TV while that twat Toby Keith
sings on the jukebox. It beggars belief,
but Saddam's "at the top of his list."
It goes on like this until late in the night.
You can say what you think, but it might mean a fight,
so you fondle your beer with your mouth closed up tight,
but your free hand closed up in a fist.

ART HOUSE CINEMA

Opening Credits

Accordion music's joined by clarinet
and then the director's name, a cityscape,
a human form, still just a silhouette.
A shot. The shadow's down. A quick escape
as the well-known actor's name bursts through the
        gloom,
followed by the girl's, though in this room,
we know the plot already, from a class
or book or film review, what to expect
from the director's work—a weekend pass,
a retrospective, and a familiar name,
a shibboleth of awe, at least respect
or reverence, the reason that we came.

Think clichés—how opposites attract,
how he met her, or how the fight was won,
the underdogs who carry the second act
with dignity—although it's in good fun.
But here, tonight, it's slightly more abstract
in black and white. And this is how we like it—
take the convention, batter it, and strike it
with something else. The opening scene's begun

on a European street
all age and shadows, early summer heat
implied by the heroine
in a svelte new sun dress, delicate and thin
as a modish cigarette
(the actress will get cancer, but not yet),
and the hero of the caper
sips coffee as he burrows through the paper
at a picturesque café—
ironic calm, since trouble's on the way.
The actor speaks his line—
subtitled, yes, but we all think that's fine
despite the bad translation
and revel in the iconic situation
and settle further in our seats to see
what lies in store for them, and you, and me.

Entr'acte

The griminess of plot and seedy bars
that dot the film like tumors as our hero
chain-smokes through misfortune, dodging cars
in search of a fortune—or reprieve?—drops out,
and as we go from racing speed to zero,
we stop for a moment near a waterfront.

The key's to always *get* it, not to pause
or linger on ideas till the end,
but focus on procedure—the swift caress
of tracking shots, the way the lights portend
significance, the slight off-kilter clause
in a sentence. It's all in the technique—
fifty years ago or just last week,
her face has stayed that oval of remorse,
her line that classic of the femme fatale
(though only understood as text, of course,
in yellow script). This is what we seek
in shadows-and-caves suggestions of celluloid:
a moving, pure alignment of it all.

Extras in the background play at cards.
The city's emptiness becomes a void
beyond established landmarks. Her and him.
Or maybe not, although they're at the center
of the shot, an alternate dimension
between the exposition of the plot
and some conclusion that will skirt convention.
But still we linger. This is the money shot,
the poster on a wall, the cultured hard-on,
the pregnant moment that the lovers part on
to be reunited only near the end
in farcical mischance that hardly matters.
Despite the car chase and the final splatter,
this is the *mise en scène* that will transcend
the train ride home, the vagaries of style.
We won't forget his shout, her rueful smile.

Closing Credits

Darkness, always darkness, at the start,
and silence till the closing credits roll.
Each one of us retreats into ourselves,
an act of solipsism for the art
of reverential silence, of control
of feelings that we cannot call our own.

Our passions stay uncooled
within our bundled clothes, and all are fooled
by silent soliloquies
that argue with the images one sees
onscreen or in the slush
of a February night. The sluggish rush
to reach the train slows down.
Is that something glowing in the brown
of a melting pile of snow?
What's *that* doing here? We don't quite know—
a cast-off cigarette
lies in a drift, smoldering and wet.
And then we walk away
to a city street, a different shade of gray,
and a static traffic jam,
and you're still you, and I'm still what I am.

LESS THAN EXPECTED

Take a breath, since this will hurt
a little less than you expect—
the promise of a trudge to work,
nights in front of the TV set,

an interest in the football match,
a furtive yearning for Miss June
that tingles upward from the crotch,
skin-rag eyes that beam disdain

though briefly, as the brain concocts
a minor victory, a spark
of sympathy that counteracts
unstated insults from the dark

that hum like crickets by the fence,
wordless in their creaking scorn,
allowing reason no defense
from accusations still half-formed

that rasp out what you never wished
while (mercifully) alone in bed,
fantasies that never washed,
the loss of what you never had.

THE ONLY THING THAT CHANGES IS THE LIGHT

We're back into the dream, on city streets
where sleepers mutter slogans as they sit
and pantomime a steering wheel while snoring
on a listless bus's upper deck.
The only thing that changes is the light.

The only thing that changes is the light
that permeates the mist we don't quite feel
though it cocoons the monuments and clothes
hanging, sodden, from our leaden limbs.
It's softer when we look from far away.

It's softer when we look from far away
and through improper lenses from an old
prescription made for slightly sharper eyes,
wide open and attentive to the flashes
blending into a glow as they recede.

Blending into a glow as they recede,
the stars dissolve to streetlights, headlights, night-lights.
We lip-synch history as we pass through
the thoroughfares that memory reroutes.
Familiar features alter into strangers'.

The only thing that changes is the light.
It's softer when we look from far away.
Blending into a glow as they recede,
familiar features alter into strangers'.

SCENESHIFTS

I

Just past the Georgian buildings, as I near
the traffic-choked bridge, I listen to the noises
that burble like bubbles rising from the river,
stagnant and stinking. Not exactly feared,
those unwashed memories, although I shiver—
and blame the cold. The sounds of far-off voices,
slightly familiar, whisper parts of phrases
that I should recognize, as unseen gazes
rake my hair—or is that just the wind?
Why do I think of you, and do I stutter
as I cross the bridge and reach its end,
breath uneven, pulse a nervous flutter?

City of absences! I tried to hold
the memory like fading rays of sun
that glisten in puddles, shifting to reflections
of headlights as the sun sets. It gets cold.
Disoriented by random interjections,
I speed up till I'm nearly at a run
and almost home in streets devoid of you,
with strangers passing and a constricted view
of steeples and a river and the stars
suffusing through city lights to reach the ground,
offset by the sound of soft guitars
filling my head with wistful wisps of sound.

Lay me down to sleep, if I can rest,
O Lady of My Memory and spread
the sheets above me, covering my face,
until the heartbeat throbbing in my chest
diminishes, and flows of dreams erase
my thoughts. Unsure if I'm asleep or dead,
and heedless of the consequences, I
will stay here, motionless, beneath a sky
both starless and unseen, a canopy
of stucco framing this, my mute repose,
and you, O Lady of My Memory,
will lie beside me as my eyelids close.

II

A shift of scene. Move forward from one stop
onto another as it's getting brighter.
The bus pulls in, and I almost drop
my cigarette while fumbling with my lighter.

"Were you the man who used to sing the songs
out on the square
for change or bags of weed
as passers-by would pause to yell requests
in other native languages—
love songs, dance songs, the news of the day?"

And silence
as memories returned that weren't mine
but anecdotes of someone else's travel,
thumb to the road, a foreign subway line,
a threadbare coat just starting to unravel.
"Jhoo are Eenglish yes?" The look ges blank.
"You've got the wrong guy." Pause. "Oh, you're the
        Yank."

Which one are you? Which woman's absent shoulder
won't support my head as I wake up wincing
and stare out the window, ever so slightly older,
memories more jumbled and unconvincing?

But the practicalities…
Did I remember to pay the parking meter,
keep my vowels up front, pronounce my R's,
lock the door, shut off the stove and heater
and cast my lot against the distant stars,
savoring the morning's cautious glow,
overdressed for as-yet-distant snow?

And a series of buses
and tourists chatting in my native tongue,
and I thought, *Dear God, have I been gone so long?*
as I shared in the distaste
for the ignorance of the timetables
and the denominations of the local currency,

and I stared
at the expanses of new estates
miles away from the anecdotes
of aging buskers.

The memories are running far away,
a squeal of tape rewinding, back to shops
stocked full of sweets, the sky a bluish gray
above an empty rugby pitch, then stops,

and for the merest fraction of a second,
a half of an iota of an instant,
I can feel her head against my shoulder,
remember fondling locks of curly hair...
and know that this is much too much to bear.

Did we break even?
Did we make out like bandits?
No, more like clumsy, eager adolescents
groping in cars, a quick ejaculation,
and crises on the family vacation.

We wondered if we still could make it back
on what was in the tank, and held on tight,
a love of necessity, a shocking lack
of exit plans within the incipient night.

And in the press of half-formed recollections,
tickets in pockets, and noisy interjections
from passengers debating their directions,
the scene shifts further as a brooding dawn
glowers above the trees, and we move on.

III

Rain. And the river, wrathful, surges
unheeded in the headiness of a half-dream night.
The living lurch in layers of the skull,
and I rise retching, wracked with the sense
of a meeting missed, a marred assignation.
Is fever at fault? The foul weather
whips past the walls, but the wind mutters,
O Muse of Memory, mother of the restless,
who delves in dreams, digging for samples
in stab-marks of stars or the stutters of phrases
I couldn't quite acquire for my tongue.

And you, who lie asleep beside the water,
alone, in company, dead drunk or sober.
Riding high, incipiently hungover,
someone's lover, someone else's daughter—
guarding the gold that rests in the riverbed
even if its gleam is false. Unseen,
it can't be turned to numbers, but instead
can only shine.

       I don't know where it's been,
what bold adventurers have sallied forth
from Hyperborean strongholds in the North
to seize it, or what gouty Nibelung
whispered nothings through his half-held breath
(not much to look at, surely, but well-hung).
But each scenario's been done to death.

Watch over me, maiden, as I drift to sleep,
and sing your arias in gentler keys,
voices like a river, flowing deep.
Alto clef, not brazen Valkyries.

IV

But here, a dashed-off note, and here, the wreck
that rises to the surface for a second,
propelled into view by violent turbulence
I cannot see. The remnants of the deck
rise at an angle.

                     But no mermaids beckoned;
someone else's filched inheritance
came to nothing. I watched from far away
as if the mess were none of my concern,
as if it were footage filmed some other day.
Type it up, then save and press Return.

Old e-mails on the screen,
and sentences no longer meant return
in pallid cyberlight, the time between
shrunk to an instant; embers start to burn.

And I must have reread those words
at least a hundred times
as the rain fell in bitch-slaps on the roof
and the frozen pizza turned brown in the oven with the
temperature set too high,
and two drunks on the street staggered by singing "The Fields
      of Athenry"
as they stuffed their faces with lukewarm chips,
and a teenaged girl, young and beautiful and aching with the
      fatal joy of being human,
pressed her middle finger to the window of the Subway shop.

Forget her
        and do better.
                  I'd forgotten
everything, except for random jetsam
that mingled in the surf, bleached out and rotten,
items that haunt you... *only if you let them.*
But I remembered, far too well, a place
no longer mine, a different port of call,
and botched itineraries, and a face
that launched some ships.
                       It wasn't that way at all.

V

Midnight; dull electric bulbs resume
their vigil over stacks of crumpled paper,
dirty dishes, an ashtray's unkempt bloom...
and memories of the way her fingers taper...

That weekend night, the music blared, its bass line thick.
I took a corner spot,
watched nubile rear-ends shaking to a Latin beat,
and ordered up a shot
then got another beer that cost me far too much.
I didn't dance at all.
I wondered if I still looked suave—or still looked thin
while sitting by the wall.
Those evenings end. They rarely go the way you'd like.
The morning doesn't care
about the disks the hipster deejay spun that night
or whether you were there.
They just let go when weekdays are too much to stand.
They buy another round
and lose themselves in dance and endless draughts of
        beer
and gushing throbs of sound.
Why can't they goddamn see the well-lit exit sign,
the reasons to mistrust
the dead end of the sensual, the awkward blink
that frames that gaze of lust?

Paracetamol. A drink of water.
A bad kebab, a wince through one last smoke.
The heat's set where it was, though it seems hotter.
I don't know why, but it's the perfect joke...

I didn't see the city much that languid week.
I barely went outside,
her head by mine, a single, narrow pillow shared,
the gratitude and pride
that she was sleeping next to me... it still seems strange,

like someone else's life,
or maybe like a thin and arid fantasy
of someone else's wife.

It's just another round you never mean
to drink, and then you find yourself outdoors,
dew on the ground—a slick and chilly sheen—
then street, then locks, familiar corridors…

Now no one's hands but mine will rearrange the sheets
in night-time tugs of war.
There's no one here to grumble at my coarser ways
or grimace at my snore,
and in the short term, I will lie awake in bed
and murmur to my pride
that this is just another stage of life, and that
I'm glad she left my side.

And heedless of the consequences, I
will stay here, motionless, beneath a sky
both starless and unseen, a canopy
of stucco framing this, my mute repose,
and you, O Lady of My Memory,
will lie beside me as my eyelids close.

SPECTRAL MORNINGS

ICE STORM

Isn't it beautiful, the way the ice
holds the streets in stasis, but with glints
that flash their warnings as cautious tires roll
between the patches? You and I both wince,
consider going out, but then think twice.
Cars skid; arms break. The season takes its toll.

We're looking out from in, or there from here,
a slight or great removal from the source
of each refracted image of the chill.
I'm over here; you're over there, of course,
and if the air is frigid, it is clear
as night goes on, glittering and still.

NO SNOW YET IN GALWAY

There's no snow yet in Galway, only mist.
"Celtic" or not, it clings to everything
like fever sweat, and even here, indoors,
swaddled in blankets, giddy from caffeine
in endless cups of tea, the damp persists.
The Corrib flows, dirt brown, into the sea.

But cut to distant relatives and news
of ice in North America, power lines
that icicles have snapped like rubber bands.
Forecasts of rain. I'm here. Another year
of watching tickers on the TV screen,
sick and groggy, coughing through the night

as others weigh the risks of being where
they're loved for no good reason, for their blood
or for their childhoods. Even if it hurts
(it always hurts somehow), the recognition
of something festering can reassure
them that they're *them* despite the distances.

No snow in Oklahoma, only ice,
covering driveways, stranding pizza guys
on half-deserted entrance ramps, while lights
flicker on and off. The e-mail brings
a blustery reproach. *You coming home?*
Thanks, but no; I think I'm staying here.

Computer screens flash on and millions max
their credit cards again to make the rush
to get to "homes" that are and aren't ours,
and in the early dark, across black ice
and slushy snow, millions of wheels will spin
as they drift homeward for the holidays.

STAYING IN

And, as in so much else, it all depends
on phones' staccato rings, or on the way
the new-cut grass looks from the street today.
In glossy magazines or calls to friends,
each blade in place is noted, with the ends
shorn neatly—and the reasons that we stay
are tidied up themselves; soft phrases sway
our sentiments. We make our tired amends.

Just staying in, it all falls into place
like forks and knives you line up side-to-side
or pillows not quite meeting on the bed—
or wrinkles working inward on your face,
an aching back, a reflex sense of pride,
and thoughts that never worm into your head.

HOMELANDS

Homelands are overrated. As the surf
molded the hillside into newer shapes
I lay beside her, somewhere on the earth,
but two floors up. Tectonic plates may scrape
against each other, but the rumbling that I heard
wasn't an earthquake, but a foreign word
that spoke of this: her own geography,
visible in the moonlight that had crept
across the sheets, described in a litany
of places and events, and on the crest
of every jurisdiction was a slogan,
a promise made and then forgotten, broken
like treaties no one ever meant to honor.
And each assertion of who she thought she was
brought further strife, and by the dawn, her manner
was militant and hostile, as the Cause
demanded her allegiance and drove me out,
a foreigner, my loyalties in doubt.

THE YEAR ZERO

So try to catch a falling star,
Crush it into dust and stuff it down a jar
And throw it far away
—Mission of Burma, "Fame and Fortune"

I

Can we zero out the clock? Guitars
and drum and bass suggest the notion's dicey.
Despite the run-down surfaces of bars,
the beams below are new. The drinks are pricey.
But isn't there a look upon the faces
of trust-fund kids belying accusations
of simulacrum, summoning the traces
of lines erased some time ago? The notions
cross bounds of class and race and generations.
The kids are kids.

We recognize the motions.
The DNA's unique, although it twists
the same old double helix, and the beat
seems to drive the blood inside our wrists
through bluish veins. The song will soon repeat
its chorus, though we can't hear every word.
And this is now, and everyone is young
and jumping up and down. It seems absurd
if you can't see it.

Everything is new?
"We've see it all before"? Oh, have we really,
or something like it—Cabaret Voltaire,
Summer of Love? Tonight, the air is chilly,
but still, the dolled-up women's arms are bare,
trying to capture in a look the feel
of being where they are, but not quite here—
a place imagined, dropped into the real,
and trying to find a graft on fallow ground,
mutating with age and dressed in better gear.
Slogans fade. The rebels come around.

II

She loved to talk about her "art." I listened,
mouthed "Tristan Tzara," and she answered, "Who?"
The bar was hot; her unclad, pale arms glistened.
Her eyes were painted. I said, "Siouxsie Sioux."
She stared at me a moment, turned away,
and chatted with her band about their label,
recording contracts, sessions in L.A.,
the audience (I gather we were fine).
The upward path is narrow and unstable.
Chaotic breaks become a chorus line.

I envied her that constant present tense,
that poise of ignorance, the sheer invention
of near-incompetence, her easy sense
of who she was, the arrogant pretension
that what you do's unique. And who was I
to stare her down with history, the hard
fact of antecedence, and a dry
account of revolutions that imploded,
the way the scions of the avant-garde
wake up one day, established and outmoded
or just washed up?

                Fuck that! Get up on stage
until the money's gone, or till the spark
burns to an ember at an older age.
The backlit lights are bright. The tone is dark.
Rock on, young lady! (What the hell's her *name*?)
Stay right here, downstairs in a downtown bar.
Don't let them tell you that you're all the same.
Don't let me tell you who I think you are.

III

We've "seen it all before," the drunk flirtation
on the sidewalk, late nights on the streets,
the blank slate of a lack of reputation,
the flat with dirty dishes, dirty sheets,
and little space for second amplifiers
in the closet packed with piles of books,
a carpet of outdated concert fliers,
a girl more beautiful than you believe
—bewitching smile and slim exotic looks—
and noble notions, though perhaps naive.

But everything we take as read is new
for someone else still unendowed with loss,
the pessimism of the longer view,
the nature of the lines they have to cross.
Some day, they switch to khakis, though chagrined,
perhaps turned rueful at their indiscretions,
now smug and overpaid and double-chinned.
Or maybe they'll look back and smile that way
one does at some now-faded recollections
of what one used to be back in the day.

WE TOOK THE WRONG STEP YEARS AGO

A CHANGE OF SEASON

A sunny girl from Northern climes,
hair and skin both honey-bright
with wide blue eyes, and in the gray
of an early spring, exuding light,

she reeks of health. Her diary
is crammed with fitness, every date
a rushed itinerary, full
of things to keep her in that state—

aerobics and organic fruit
—rip the flesh and suck the pips!—
bike to work from a D4 home...
until one day, her bright gaze slips

and falls on him, Italianate—
subtle, with a hint of threat,
bling on his finger. And his voice
cloys with a charm that makes her wet.

So he's "in business"—various things—
the sort of wealth with wads of cash
from nowhere in particular,
a sleek Mercedes, and a stash

of blow from South America
back at his place (with potpourri
above the toilet, and the sink
crowned with mousses from Italy).

Fast-forward through frenetic nights,
romantic dinners, snorted coke,
flowers delivered to her work,
their favorite song, their private joke.

He takes the gambit, and succeeds.
A ring's produced, and she says yes
on a long walk through Phoenix Park.
The wind is blowing from the west,

wafting and dulcet, as the sun
sinks down behind the stands of trees,
promising in a breathless rush
a life of indolence and ease.

But still, they pack and make their way
to meet the "Family," now hers,
with bodyguards and smoking wives
with Gucci bags and hideous furs.

Proserpina looks up and gasps,
stupid in her shock, her scream
unuttered as they pull her down,
beyond the reeking, corpse-choked stream

burbling with the failing pleas
that echo through the dark and wet,
rushing into darker caves
beyond forgiveness or regret.

WHITE ANGLO-SAXON PROTESTANT

Wilson saw it in the celluloid—
a nation purified in stark white sheets.
The newsreel ends; the storyline repeats:
There's always something left to be destroyed
with ropes or bags of cash or with Marines
who charge up hillsides. Flags are planted. Scene.

My Grandpa was a Kraut, just like his Dad.
Rednecks used to beat his ass while prating
that these here parts don't take no hyphenating.
"Don't like it, Fritz? Well, that's too goddamn bad.
You're one of us!" By God, it's still amazing
what you can do with vigilante hazing.

He had no choice but make a choice—and did.
Never learning his parents' speech, he merged
into the English-speaking world as urged
by the local thugs. But even as he hid
behind a surname that he mispronounced,
war ended, yet his lineage stayed renounced.

A proxy WASP, a diplomatic move
worthy of von Clausewitz, the stench
of total war progressing inch by inch
flowing through our veins. What does it prove?
Well, not a goddamn thing, but all you need
to know. Shut up and find a girl and *breed.*

And as I stood by Great-Great Grandma's grave
—"geboren" and "gestorben" etched in stone—
I could feel the marrow in each bone
hum with a hymn I didn't know, each wave
of unheard sound a dirge of dispossession.
Close the KJV. Here ends the lesson.

THE LEAP

If I am capable of grasping God objectively, I do not believe,
but precisely because I cannot do this I must believe.

—Søren Kierkegaard

It's not the fall that acrophobics fear,
the fatal inattention, as the body
accelerates, and distant crawling figures
whirring on the ground gain features, voice,
reflex cacophonies of screams and honking
as the concrete of the street approaches.

They fear the jump itself, the narrow ledge
bordering a moist and chilly sky,
the moment when a day like any other
picks up speed and plunges into space
that's always there, in lungs and hair and eyes,
but only now regarded for itself,

beyond immense, its endless grandeur felt
despite its invisibility, the shape
of fronts that spread across the continent
in forms that only metaphor reveals
in lines and arrows on a map. Out there,
the sky is palpable; the gusts are strong.

The realization gives but little comfort
until, despite the snap of wind, they sense
their feet against the ground again, the air
the merest pockets in the curving arches
between the toes that dig into their socks
and heels that swivel, testing what's below.

IT'S BUSINESS

We now assume a playing field
with level ground and unconcealed

goals and borders, with a ref
who isn't on the take, or deaf.

But no such luck. The same old fix
against the rednecks from the sticks

still operates behind the bleachers,
admin halls, impassive features,

with club ties hidden under sweaters
so no one really knows one's "betters"

and cannot know the game's been thrown,
but thinks it's down to skill alone.

JIMMY CARTER, KING OF AMERICA

I must have been—what?—four when Jimmy Carter
stepped out of Air Force One on the TV set,
smiling and shaking hands despite the polls
and all the shit that must've been going down.
There were exorcisms in Tehran,
with "Death to the Great Satan!" on the lips
of mullahs, while the Soviet helicopters
swarmed Afghanistan. But I was four
and didn't know quite who the hell it was
waving at us, so I asked my mom.

"That's Jimmy Carter, Quincy." But who's he?
"The leader of our country." Oh, our *king*.
I'd heard the fairy tales and thought I knew
the ins and outs of war and politics.
But he didn't look that regal in a suit
like something that my dad would wear to church.
No crown or scepter—and what was with the surname?
Kings had numbers, or really awesome titles
like "Lionheart," "the Mad," "the Third," "the Bold,"
"the Great"—or even "the Magnificent."

I went outside and played catch with my dad,
who laughed when I explained what I had learned
about our king. But grown-ups always laughed
(or so it seemed) at my discoveries—
that the sky was far too high to reach,
even for them, that toilet water swirled
the same direction every time you flushed,
that snow was frozen rain. I let him laugh,
and then my dad and I went in to eat
the supper that was always on the table.

King Carter was replaced by Ronald Reagan—
who had a different last name, and was older.
I learned about elections, the tradition
of voting on a Tuesday for our leaders—
all citizens "like us." But soon enough,
I heard of Contras out in jungles, islands
swarming with Marines... and slavery,
homeless people, and laid-off auto workers,
and that our TV came from far away,
a place whose name I couldn't quite pronounce.

You can't go back, of course. The TV set
is in some dump in central Oklahoma.
A different generation's in the yard
of the house my mother sold when she dumped Dad.
I've also learned that you don't need a king
to have an empire, court, and sycophants
while the poor get screwed, and every day, the news
comes like a tedious joke, in sober suits,
straight-faced insanity that we switch off,
then heat a frozen dinner from the fridge.

TRIPTYCH

Saturday Morning

The driving scourge, the contour of the flesh
that, flayed past any wisdom, turns to mush,
the sudden surge of wounds exposed afresh;
they lead to ruptures. As the fissures gush,

Bathsheba's bastards from the illicit tumble
will stare at shadows, too fucked-up and frightened
to keep their act together, let things crumble,
and leave the kingdom weakened, unenlightened.

His clothing crumpled by the mantelpiece
seems to rustle slightly with his snore
that echoes with a vacuous release.
Though no one's there, she glances at the door.

And now she turns to stare at the pictures on
the mantel, disarrayed by last night's passion,
disturbed or just knocked over as the dawn
approached—but a progression in a fashion.

A dark-haired little girl, with all the schmaltz
of knee-length dresses, ponytails, and dolls,
a gap-toothed smile that doesn't (yet) seem false...
or maybe a tomboy dressed in overalls

with Tonka truck in hand. A ballerina?
A Daddy's Girl? A miniature of Mom?
A gymnast aiming for the sports arena?
A future heartbreak waiting for her prom?

A picture's static image can't reveal
the uncommemorated days—nor can it
capture in light the way she used to feel
some day beneath the sun on this blue planet.

The past is breached; the front collapses in.
She grasps his hand, a gesture faked by rote,
rehearsed in daydreams, wheedled out with gin.
A rumbling noise comes belching from his throat.

The neighbors note the unfamiliar car
and wonder how their property will smell
when downwind from the backwash of the bar.
His car's up on the curb, parked parallel

the burglar of the body shifts and farts.
He gets up, staggers off, and urinates.
She groans, and her defenses come apart
like shredded cocktail napkins, but she waits

for him to come to bed to throw him out.
Shock ricochets across his face. He rises,
dresses, holding back a furious shout
against the "fucking bitch." He leaves. The crisis

is done for now, until another night,
another business trip that leaves her stranded,
lonely, and bored, with ravenous appetite
for some companionship, cajoled, demanded—

with the same results. Convenient fictions,
raw material for the shrink next week—
catharsis, yes, but mixed with dark predictions
of too much booze, a passable physique.

It does no good when he has gone away
to say it didn't happen. Nonetheless,
she sets those thoughts aside, and through the day,
the light streams in; she watches motionless.

And where the hell's Uriah as she moans
another's name (or was it his?) in bed—
"off on business"? Even though he phones—
she knows his mind is somewhere else instead

perhaps his job and keeping her in style
while keeping far away to play at power
in conference rooms. She'll bear it for a while,
but waits for David to see her in the shower.

Saturday Afternoon

The chic cafe in the poshest shopping center,
a caramel macchiato and a paper,
while strains of some obese Italian tenor
stir in the background. But his arias taper

into some singer with a soft guitar.
The CD's at the counter, and her friends
shift the conversation to the star
they barely hear. The tangent hits its end,

then on to the news and gossip and the kids
that Katie hasn't had, persistent rumors
that she'd hit—and here I quote—"the skids."
Innuendoes metastasize like tumors.

The sagging eyelids give it all away,
the fumble for her purse, the murmured hex
against the brightness of this Saturday
afternoon. A subtle stench of sex

clings to her body like cologne. She shifts
self-consciously beneath their judging gazes,
narrowed with knowing, and by the time she lifts
the coffee to her lips, the staring blazes.

"Are you coming to the benefit?"
Yeah right. They have to ask. Recall the scene
last winter? Then they're talking baby shit,
God knows what else. How to keep things clean

without the hired help. And what was that?
Yes, it's Dior, and yes it's new. I know
you only mean to say I'm getting fat.
But you can't say these things out loud. God, no.

The etiquette of malice is quite subtle,
especially served cold, reduced to craft,
shrewd as diplomacy. Emotions scuttle
the delicate interplay upon a raft

of those who tolerate each other. School
or charities or work; it doesn't matter.
Each has its own, unstated Golden Rule.
"Do unto others..."? Bullshit! Stick to chatter,

never show weakness. Don't come out and say it,
insinuate. And never show your hand
but damn well know how you intend to play it,
aggressive and ruthless, eager for command.

Sunday Evening

And there she is, a model for us all,
brunette and buxom, eyes widely set and blue,
wasp waist, long legs, ever so slightly tall,
the stuff of songs. And what's a man to do

except applaud? This woman's our ideal,
a huge collective hard-on, and we see her
emerge from the contestants, almost real,
as also-rans exhale and want to be her...

drunk and spoken for and slightly mad,
a strapless gown but frumpy underwear,
weeping as the scene turns mopey-sad—
tragic or pathetic, do we care?

Well, not tonight. The moral is the same
as it is every night, at home or out,
alone or with another. Sobs of shame
from well-known sources follow every bout

till she collapses, sick, unsatiated,
into a pillow with a lusty snore.
Turn out the lights, angry but sedated.
Head for the couch and softly close the door.

The nights are cold despite the thermostat,
the duvet that she wraps up around her feet.
The nights are always dark despite the flat
outside glimmers—pale, devoid of heat.

"It's hard being beautiful"; the expectations
prove too much sometimes, and so she rests
swathed in blankets against these situations,
arms crossed defensively beneath her breasts

against intruders, husbands, and such lovers
as come her way. It's much more cozy here
behind the door and underneath the covers.
Repeat, repeat. There goes another year.

A few more hairs turn gray; a few more lines
crinkle from her eyes; a bit more sag
lowers her bosom. An old dress underlines
a thin expanse of flab. But still, she'll brag

about the pictures on the mantelpiece,
a woman she resembles, but never was.
She'll pay a shrink to rant to for "release,"
trying to figure out the things that cause

her to be like this, but in the night,
there's just recrimination as the drink
recedes, and fears of age and cellulite
take over. *Screw it. Tell it to your shrink*

if you'll feel better, but I'm through with you,
your false "new starts." That tragic diva pose,
the things you weep—even when they're true.
Hangovers wait beneath the pile of clothes.

WATCHER OF THE SKIES

OUT OF SHOT

Outside the window, different shades of light
imply the movements of other lives. A car
screeches into action in the lot.
The rails on the beds, the IV drips,
and light blue gowns sequester us from *them,*
dressed in their daytime civvies, late for work,
fumbling with car keys—we can't hear the jingle
or muttered curses at cacophonous
alarm clocks on the bed stands we can't see.

We see a bit, of course, from where we are
and know what's going on beyond our sight.
The window, pigeon dropping-smeared, lets in
a limited tableau, a TV screen
without commercial interruption, cast
with nothing but extras, a wide, extended shot
without a zoom to close-up—since the star
of the series is convalescing off the screen
and watching from a bed that's not his own.

HEUSTON STATION

But as the train pulled out, the sun was shining,
though cautiously—a woman's guarded smile
at some weak play of humor. Silver lining?
No. Perhaps a respite for a while
in a land of drizzle and too many queues,
resentful songs of rebels long since beaten,
an awful shrink-wrapped sandwich still uneaten,
and evenings killed off with too much booze.

WE ALL HAVE OUR NEEDS

I watch two twentysomethings on the train
and know what's on their minds, their faces stuck
in cautious non-expression as their brains
grow giddy with their unexpected luck.
But why suppress their feelings? There's no shame
in wanting it, in getting some at last,
a little closer with each station passed—
a gonad's urge that no one needs to name.

But when you score, something always slips
from balled-up sheets, from minds, from frenzied lips.
And past the press of chests and groins and hair
a silence settles—trumping everything
that you can say, or hold to, even cling
against yourself—and saturates the air.

MINOR CHARACTER

The bit-part actor takes a hurried drag,
stubs the cigarette with a velvet shoe,
and makes his entrance from stage left to say,
"Clubs, bills, and partisans! strike! beat them down!
Down with the Capulets! down with the Montagues!"
First Citizen's speech is over. Exeunt.
The scene's been set. The actor heads backstage
then has a whiskey in the bar next door.

Four acts to go on stage. We know the plot,
the balcony, the swooning, the belated
realization the Citizen was right—
although he's gone and long since out of costume,
faded into anonymity,
the greater, uncommemorated suffering.

THE REST OF THE STORY

There is no cause but this—a speeding train,
a damsel on the track. But it's not clear
why she was hog-tied as the train grew near,
or why the hero dashed across the plain,
all sweat and streaming hair. And did the villain
want her money, did he want revenge,
or what the hell's the story? Who will fill in
the damned ellipses? Therein lies the tinge
of bias, pious declarations, stock
melodrama, studies in archetype,
varying degrees of smut and hype,
specifics added in for added shock,
piano players plunking through a score
of tunes we know by heart, our certitude
the girl's, the hero's. He'll be back for more
next week, his hair in place, his methods crude.

IF GOD IS GOOD

If God is good, and if the weather holds,
and if the horse comes in, we might allow
a glint of teeth between a face's folds—
a smile that promises, at least for now,
that God is good, and that the weather holds.

If life is chance, if chaos is our lot,
and if the math can't quite be reconciled
—even with itself—then what we've got
is probability. But dice fly wild,
since life is chance, and chaos is our lot.

If she were near, and I could hear the sound
of placid breathing up against my ear,
her reassuring sleep might bring to ground
the migratory urge that brought me here
if she were near, if I could hear the sound.

If God were good, and if the sky stayed blue,
and she were here, and all the numbers fit,
and all the things that I believe were true,
would I notice, even for a bit,
that God is good, and that the sky stays blue?

A PLAGUE OF LIGHTHOUSE KEEPERS

THE NEWS COMES EVERY MORNING

Another day in waiting rooms. The doctor eyes the suture,
then bills you for a thousand bucks—says, "Think about the
    future."
The nurses smell of Calvin Klein, the waiting room of whiskey.
We stagger into taxicabs, our faces green and frisky.

I gave my love a cherry, and it floated in the cocktail.
We chatted till the bars were closed and broke it off by e-mail.
I gave my love a dining set. I gave my love a chicken.
She smothered it in flour and eggs, and so our waistlines
    thicken.

The news comes every morning, and the news is always bad.
The men on television smirk while slowly going mad.

A rumor spreads by radio, infecting like a virus
till counter-rumors put it down. It rises like Osiris,
twice as strong and tough as hell in its present incarnation.
I listened in a groggy haze, and then I switched the station.

We gave up dreams of second cars, of porches and cyclone
    fences,
of farting out the aftermath of coffee and cheese blintzes,
of jobs downtown and mortgages on houses in the valley—
all for a lurid fantasy of blowjobs in an alley.

The news comes every morning, but the morning's history
like pyramids, trench warfare, and the "new economy."

William Montgomery went to work, then blew his monthly
    paycheck
on a Nudie Cohen outfit made of sequins and white spandex.
Katie saw him and laughed so hard she gurgled through the
    bourbon
she sipped while she was driving home in her new gray
    Suburban.

Bill Clinton sucked—but didn't inhale—the tail end of a reefer,
served his time, serviced the girls, then floated into ether.
Hillary looked at the latest polls and threw away the paper.
"I might be sagging around the eyes, but at least I'm not Ralph
    Nader."

The news comes every morning, and the news is always brisk,
a ticker on the TV screen, a download saved to disk.

Someone's won a TV set; someone's won the Booker;
someone's won a million bucks on *Are You a Pirate Hooker?*
Someone's scared of rabid dogs; someone's scared of Satan;
someone's in his dad's garage, rocking to Van Halen.

You can crack equations; you can calculate the function
and end up scanning horoscopes for a distant star's
    conjunction.
You can buy insurance; you can keep away from matches
but still, one day the lightning strikes and burns the place to
    ashes.

APARTMENTS

No ghosts as yet, but just a hint of fever
(the fan's still in its box) and foreign noise.
A virgin phone squats on its new receiver.
Undusty window sills are bare but ready
for clocks, for brown, anemic plants, their poise
temporary, fragile and unsteady.

There have been other places, across the river,
or oceans, time zones—other furniture,
with curtains cutting light to just a sliver,
those old apartments populated still
with women whom you recollect as "her."
They haven't called; you doubt they ever will.

Each lease becomes an act of... not forgetting,
but somehow letting go. Old places live
with different faces in a familiar setting:
lives you'll never know, but comprehend,
scenes of errors not yours to forgive,
broken hearts no longer yours to mend.

MASKS

So stark, the sky above the railroad track!
It washes out all color, blends to gray
the vacant, gazing faces and the black
of newsprint filled with murders blocks away.

So cold, the scowls of strangers on the train!
Suspicious eyes glance over headlines full
of cries for vengeance; pupils seem to strain
against a tunnel's gloom. Beyond control

or commonplace restraint, a vision shows
the crooked teeth and cleaving tongue of spite
that hiss in crowded spaces. Heaven knows
their hooded, hungry looks in bars at night

filled full with false good fellowship in clots
of co-conspirators, who pant and glare
at snaking rows of newly emptied shots
and women with a vapid, reptile stare.

SUICIDE TOWN

i.m. Ray Pospisil

Across the city, computer screens flash on—
in Brooklyn brownstones, littered sties of dorms,
Midtown offices, and Inwood flats.
Another day begins, a steely blue,
and we're above it, talking to ourselves
in tones of clacking keyboard strokes, our eyes
straining at the missives that we write
to cyberspace, expecting no reply.

Suicide town! Where unsung poets write
quarterly reports or articles
about the latest merger in Japan
or theses on the recent politics
of places that they fled to end up here—
bored, with just a screen for company.

New York, New York! Or Staten Island, Queens,
the Bronx, or Brooklyn, and far too many trains
with suicide lighting flickering on faces
until we look like corpses in the gloom,
pallid, with a laminate of sweat
glistening as we slump against the seats.

Sunset. Jersey glowers to the west.
Apartments echo a cacophony
of daydreams, words of love we only speak
into a pillow, and the tangled plots
of novels still unwritten, while our lives
are lived alone—and lonely—like a farce
without the comedy, until we slip,
drunk and murmuring, into our beds.

YE WATCHERS AND YE HOLY ONES

Cold comfort, yes, that last descending line
that sinks into the rafters and the pews,
a seeming Pyrrhic triumph over death
that comes like backaches or the evening news
as we move on. A million lights will shine
against the empty sea.
                  We hold our breath,
or hold our loved ones. Cling with all our might!
Cling to unproven promises, the trust
that neither side has earned, although each must
preserve the proper forms and get it right.

Pause as the organ drones; the coalescence
of images and faces and abstraction
is broken by a cough, our very essence—
a sickly rasp, a faint, half-hearted action.

A fallacy, perhaps, and Lazarus
lies decomposed and stinking, while the stone
stays in its place. Neither alive nor dead,
we face that old uncertainty, alone
and in the outer darkness, each of us
pretending that we somehow hold the thread
that leads us out of here.
                A murmured prayer
recalls a song and others who have passed
this way before. We wonder, at the last,
if other voices fill the rustling air.

BROOKLYN, 2008

I

We've plunged to winter. Economic graphs
    show more troughs than peaks
and promise further chills ahead
    in the coming weeks.
Sales are down. The stores are cutting prices,
    although to small avail.
Bills foreshadowing repo men
    show up in the mail.

Still, Christmas shoppers mill in Fulton Mall,
    and out in Prospect Park,
the yuppies follow happy dogs
    until the sky gets dark,
until the weather drops a bit too much,
    until the rent increases,
until the insurance won't pay up
    when faced with new diseases.

You'd think there'd have to be a protest march
    with banners—or a riot.
There's a light breeze in the Heights;
    in Park Slope, all seems quiet.
And only stops away in Williamsburg,
    the bars stay open late,
spilling out their bright young things
    in a fragile, altered state.

The psychiatric trade is always brisk.
    In little rooms, like priests,
they listen. We confess our sins,
    and for a time at least,
it's figured out, until the week's events
    circle to a chair
and soothing prints along the wall
    and a sympathetic stare.

And in that office, stammered sentences
    flow as the thoughts cohere—
the low-key power-plays at work,
    the shrapnel of a year
spent dodging each misfortune that arrives
    in this wave or the next—
 company memos, budget cuts,
    the unmoved fairer sex.

Back on the subway, headphones set to stun
    echo with the crash
of waves of sound against the ear,
    quicker than the lash
of ebbs and flows of eyes that scan the ads
    plastered on the train.
Learn English! Start a New Career!
    Do You Suffer Pain?

But where's the toll-free number you can call
    when it gets cold and wet
or to check the status of a dream
    that's come to nothing yet?
The tide recedes into a half-read book,
    then breaks on strangers' faces,
back and forth, though we believe
    somehow, we're going places.

II

You're in a multiplex and wondering
    how it came to this—
beautiful people making love
    in cinematic bliss,
their shyness overcome. And all is grand
    until a second act
of obstacles soon overcome.
    You want your money back.

Back on the city street, it's still December.
    The sun's in short supply
as armies of overcoats go past.
    (The film's set in July.)
And somewhere, someone's working on a tan,
    and sometimes love's enough,
and someone's blonde, and someone's rich...
    but someone's life is rough,

and someone's house, foreclosed, is up for sale
    and someone's out of work.
A frenzied crowd has crushed the life
    out of a Walmart clerk,
trampled like a wrapper from a candy bar
    sticking to a shoe
as busy patrons rushed the shelves.
    What did you *think* they'd do?

Snarl at the cold and thrust a fist of coins
    at a gibbering bum,
get home, jerk off, and go to sleep
    before you, too, succumb
to the dissipation of a summer sky
    seen on celluloid.
The feeling lingers, though it shifts,
    soon to be redeployed.

And anyway, we all know what is what,
    and that the girls who grin
at you on platforms don't quite lie,
    but like their men more thin—
or muscular, or maybe not a stranger
    leaning against the glass.
They'll get off before your stop.
    Sigh. "This, too, shall pass."

It always passes, with the reassurance
    that she's "not your type,"
all mascara, heels, and blush,
    some bullshit market hype.
The "break-up," then, was strictly "mutual"
    —although you never spoke—
and never would have, anyway.
    She wouldn't like your jokes.

All the same, the luxury of scorn
    is some small blessing still,
a sign of better things to come,
    or maybe of "free will,"
a sense that we remain in some control
    of bank accounts and crushes
despite the crash of markets, and
    the squeeze of Christmas rushes.

III

Yesterday's headline: *Jobless Figures Surge.*
　　The market's in a drought,
bringing on a greater thirst.
　　Best spend the weekend out
and waffle on exhibits at the Met
　　or recent politics,
post-it notes of conversation.
　　Let's hope something sticks.

Friends and strangers sitting at the bar
　　with ready, cutting quips
blend into the soundscape, till
　　the jukebox CD skips,
and as a chord resounds *ad infinitum,*
　　all the chatter stops.
The barman programs in a track.
　　New song, from the top.

The women are all beautiful and bright;
　　the men are fit and clever.
We'll all be ploughed by closing time.
　　For now, it holds together
like pop song lyrics of *non sequiturs;*
　　but isn't it "ironic,"
posing as poised and debonair
　　with another gin and tonic?

Hangover. Just the standard easy fix
　　of aspirin and food,
of diner coffee drunk in sips,
　　the thought that life is good,
butter-soaked waffles, and a Spanish song
　　with an upbeat refrain,
sustaining the smug certainty
　　that you'll be here again.

And as the feeling lurking in the pain
    oozes out bit by bit,
you wonder why you do it, though
    nobody gives a shit—
and nor do you, despite the second thoughts
    that came, too late, at seven.
You've moved on to the sausages
    and swear that this is heaven.

We hurt because we can, not since we must—
    the difference is essential,
a fine distinction in the end
    but somehow fundamental
to all those bar tabs on the credit card,
    the freely flowing cash,
the love affair with the ATM,
    the mouth silted through with ash.

But as the headache dulls into a throb,
    the headline comes in clearer,
the same thing as the day before,
    ever so slightly nearer.
So take another aspirin and gulp
    your orange juice and pray
that the bill will not come due
    between now and Saturday.

IV

Bless the false dawn of a tunnel's gloom,
    the train just out of sight,
the blaze of headlights, the screech of brakes,
    the way our eyes alight
at the seemingly infernal glow.
    No. Blink. Expel the thought
like papers in a bin, a fleeting flash
    of details we forgot

somewhere between the bagel and the beer,
    between a boomed hello
and that goodbye we parted on.
    Stand up. It's time to go,
not into sunset or uncertain dawn,
    but (odd!) a sort of prayer,
chants mingling in a muted hum
    and lingering in the air.

We'll leave the train and start our ambles home
    in mobile meditation
as words congeal with clear intent
    but uncertain punctuation.
And if the phrases crumple into sound
    and ricochet off curbs
like rubbish tossed aside by drunks,
    we shouldn't be disturbed.

The night will give way soon enough to sounds
    of car alarms and voices
drowning out the subtler noise
    of our dubious choices
and second guesses of the two-room flats
    for which we pay the rent
or calculations of the cash
    waiting to be spent.

And blessed be you, despite this empty hour,
   wherever you might be—
awake in other time zones, or
   scant blocks away from me.
And if we haven't spoken, I recall
   an obsolete address.
I clutch the phone and pantomime
   the numbers that I'd press.

The number's doubted, leave it to tomorrow.
   Leave it *now*, full stop
and paragraph. Get through the door
   and take it from the top.
Brush your teeth; retreat into your bed,
   and think of gentler things—
the wondrous quiddity of day
   the morning always brings.

The context's staked out just beyond the door,
   a cop with an angry frown—
without a warrant, but still alert
   for when one's guard goes down.
Leave the thought unspoken, save in dreams
   that float out past the docks
like ships (or trash?) to far away—
   or founder on the rocks.